DINOBIBI
SINGAPORE
TRAVEL FOR KIDS

© Copyright 2019 - **Dinobibi:** All rights reserved. No part of this publication may be reproduced, stored in retrieval systems, or transmitted by any means, including electronic, mechanical, photocopying, or otherwise, without prior written permission of the publisher and copyright holder. **Disclaimer:** Although the author and Dinobibi have taken all reasonable care in preparing this book, we make no warranty about the accuracy or completeness of its content and, to the maximum extent permitted, disclaim all liability arising from its use.

CONTENTS

Introduction (pg. 4)

Geography of Singapore (pg. 6)

Weather (pg. 13)

History (pg. 16)

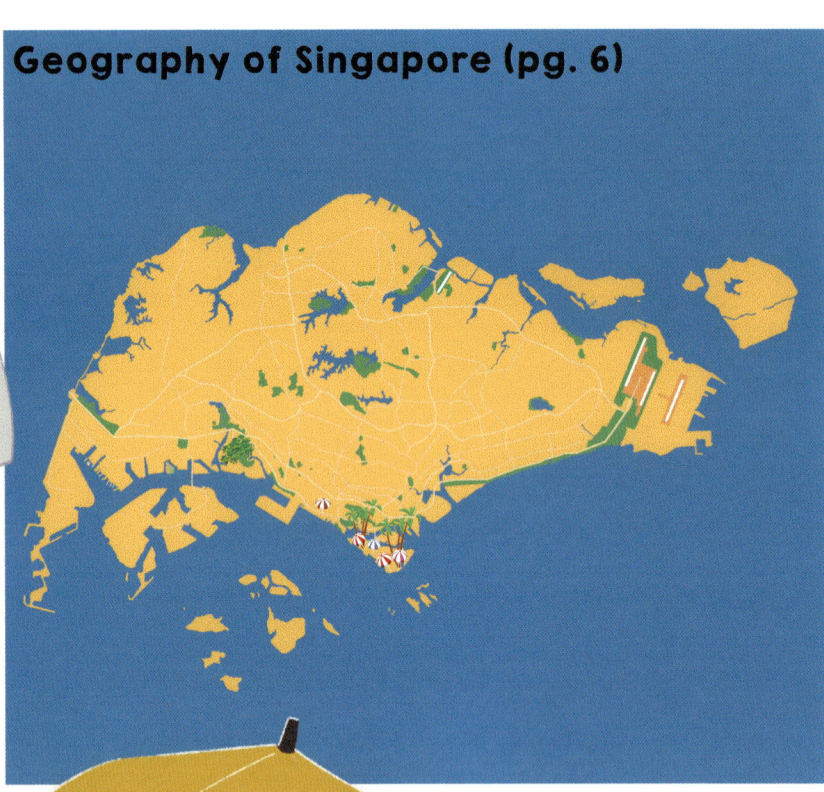

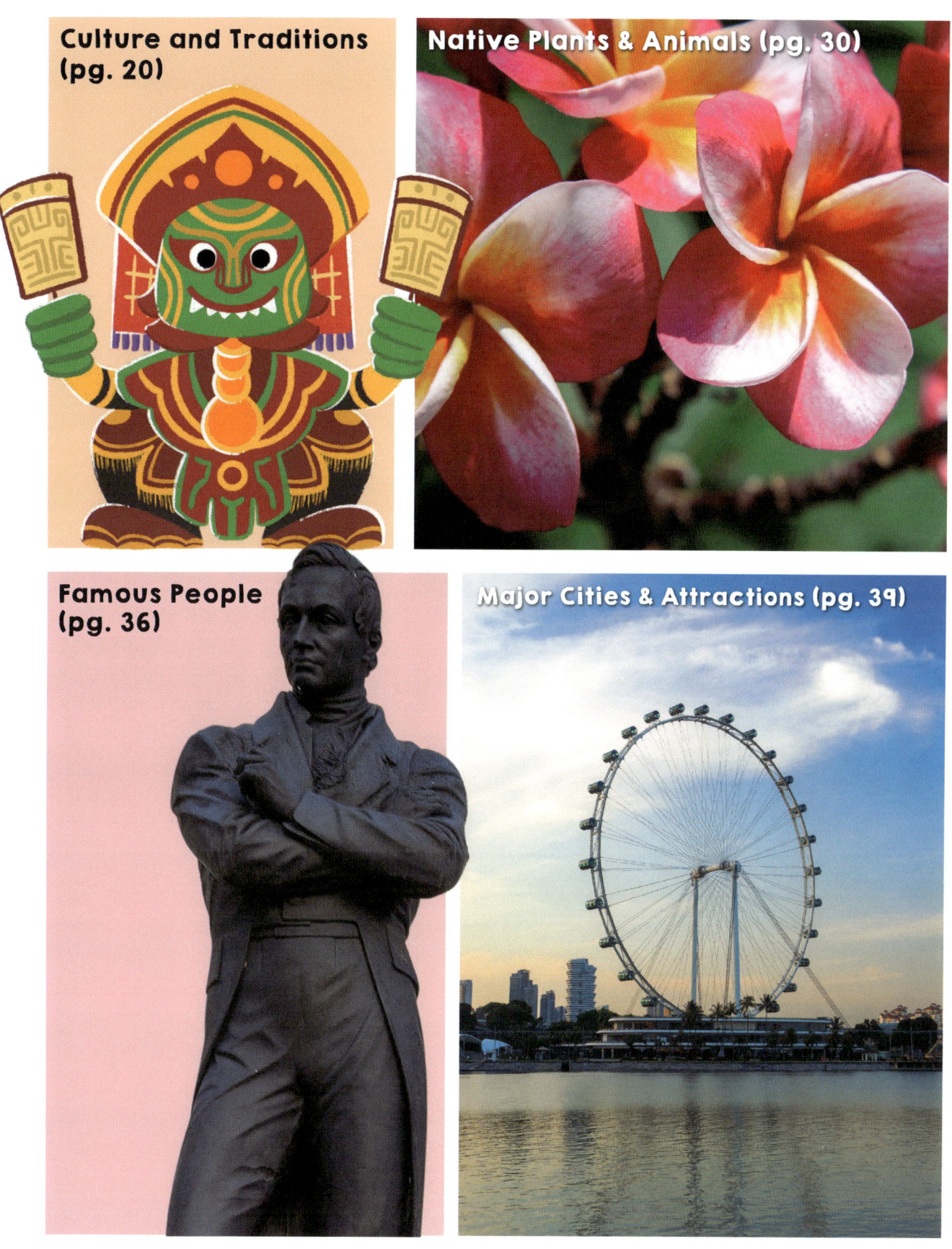

INTRODUCTION: HELLO FRIENDS!

Hello! Welcome to Singapore! I'm Bryan, a 10-year-old boy, living in Singapore. I am going to take you on a trip through my beautiful, modern country and show you all there is to see here.

Now, let me tell you more about myself. I go to a primary school in my neighborhood. At 10, I have already completed 8 years of schooling: 4 years of pre-primary and 4 years of primary school.

Singaporeans take education very seriously, and parents spend a lot of money to send us to the best of schools and tuition centers. I am proud to say that our education system is considered to be one of the best in the world.

The school year for primary schools is from January to November with one month of holidays in summer, usually in June. In addition to English, which is the primary language in Singaporean schools, we have to learn a second language as well. We can choose from Malay, Mandarin, and Tamil as our second language. So, enough about me. Let me tell you more about my country.

Now that I've told you about myself, can you please tell me the following details about you?

Your name: Poppy

Which country are you from: England

Who are you traveling with? Mum Dad brother ME!

Which places in Singapore are you most exicited about? Why? Night time zoo because it sounds ^soso exiting!

CHAPTER 1
GEOGRAPHY OF SINGAPORE

Singapore got its name from a Sanskrit word 'Singapura' which translates to 'lion city.' Sanskrit is an ancient Indian language which is still in use today.

Yes, the entire country of Singapore is made up of 63 islands and most of them are uninhabited. Apart from the main island, which is diamond-shaped, the largest ones are Sentosa, Pulau Ubin, Pulau Tekong, St. John's Island, and Sisters' Islands.

In the north, the main island of Singapore is separated from the Malaysian Peninsula by Johor Strait. A freeway and railway bridge over this strait connects Singapore to Malaysia.

In the south, Singapore Strait separates the island-country from the archipelago of Riau-Lingga, which is part of Indonesia.

The Land Relief in Singapore

Almost two-thirds of Singapore is flat land, and the highest peak, Timah Hill, is only 162 m (531 feet) above sea level. Timah Hill, Mandai Hill, Panjang Hill along with other small peaks form a rugged mountain range in the middle of the island. The soil in Singapore is not very fertile. Singapore is highly urbanized, and very little forest cover remains on the island.

Rivers in Singapore

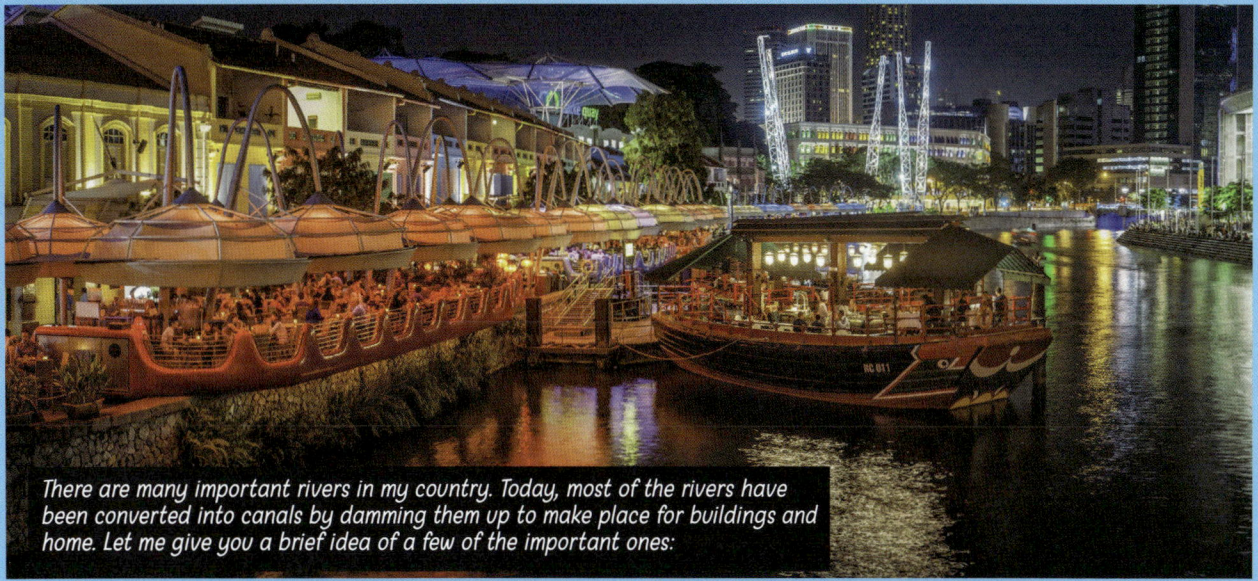

There are many important rivers in my country. Today, most of the rivers have been converted into canals by damming them up to make place for buildings and home. Let me give you a brief idea of a few of the important ones:

Geylang River — Flowing from Geylang to Kallang through the central part of the main Singapore Island, this river empties into the Kallang Basin close to Singapore Indoor Stadium.

Pandan River — Beginning in Bukit Batok and emptying into the sea at the West Coast Pier, this river is on the west coast of Singapore.

Singapore River — This river flows right through the downtown area of Singapore and empties into Marina Bay.

Kallang River — Running for over 10 km (6.2 miles), Kallang River is the longest in Singapore, starting from the Lower Pierce Reservoir and emptying into the Kallang Basin. The river and the surrounding areas are named after the native fisherfolk called biduanda orang kallang. Today, only about a 1,000 of these natives are here.

Singapore is an island city-state-country in Asia and is located off the southern coast of Malaysia, close to the southern tip of the Malaysian Peninsular. How many islands are part of the country of Singapore?

1. 3
2. 50
3. 63 ✓

(Answer – 3. 63)

Lakes in Singapore

Jurong Lake — Built mainly as a secondary water resource for the city-state of Singapore, today, this lake is a great tourist spot for both locals and international travelers. The Jurong Lake Park around it was built in 2006, which houses a Chinese-themed garden and a Japanese-themed garden.

Symphony Lake — Symphony Lake is one of three beautiful artificial lakes in Singapore Botanic Gardens. A huge stage called the Shaw Foundation Symphony Stage sits on a little islet right in the middle of the Symphony Lake.

Mountains in Singapore

Here are the top five mountain peaks in Singapore:

Bukit Timah Hill — At an altitude of 537 feet, Bukit Timah Hill is the highest mountain peak in Singapore. This peak is surrounded by Bukit Timah Nature Reserve Park, which houses nearly 40% of the island country's plants and animals.

Bukit Timah Hill is primarily made up of granite. In the 1900s, tigers roamed in the wild forests around this hill. The first person to climb the summit of this hill was the Resident Councilor of Singapore, John Prince, in 1827. He and his team of contractors reached the summit in five hours. In 1843, an access road to the peak was built. During World War II, both the Japanese and British tried to take control of Bukit Timah Hill because of its strategic location. Many military battles are known to have taken place here.

Bukit Batok — Bukit in the Malayan language is 'hill.' Batok has several connotations and some of them are:

People believed that a lot of coconut trees used to grow on this hill, and the Javanese word for coconut is 'batok.'

In Malay, 'batok' translates to granite, and since this hill is made of granite, it is named Bukit Batok.

The Bukit Batok is famous for the first television transmission tower of Singapore.

Henderson Waves bridge on Mount Faber rainforest.

Mount Faber — The earlier name of Mount Faber was Telok Blangah Hill, is about 105 meters (344 ft.) in height, and is a great place for walking and trekking. The Faber Point here gives you a 360-degree view of Singapore.

Mount Serapong — The second largest island in Singapore, Sentosa Island, houses Mount Serapong, which holds historical ruins and plenty of mysterious, dark tunnels and passageways. Another name for Mount Serapong is:

1. Clement Hill ✓
2. Mount Sentosa
3. Mount Temasek

(Answer – 1. Clement Hill)

Flag of Singapore

The flag of Singapore was adopted in 1959 along with the National Anthem and National Emblem. The rectangular flag has two broad strips: one red on top and one white on bottom.

On the left on the red strip, there is a white crescent moon and five stars. The crescent moon reflects the image of a young, developing nation. The five stars stand for the most important ideas of my country namely peace, democracy, progress, equality, and justice.

National Anthem of Singapore

The National Anthem of Singapore is 'Majulah Singapura.' In all schools, singing the national anthem in the morning assembly is a daily ritual. So, by the time we complete the first year of our primary, we have already learned memorized it!

Here are some interesting facts about our national anthem:

- Zuber Said, a Singaporean originally from Indonesia, composed the anthem.

- The entire lyrics are printed on the 1000 dollar currency note. On the other notes, only the name of the anthem is printed.

National Emblem of Singapore

The National Emblem of Singapore was adopted in 1959 and has a lion and a tiger standing on rice stalks and holding a shield. The shield has the crescent moon and the five stars on it just like how it is on the flag.

A blue ribbon is underneath the emblem, which has the words, 'Majulah Singapore' on it, which is not only the name of our national anthem, but also the country's motto.

Other National Symbols of Singapore

National animal — The national 'animal' of Singapore is the mythical Merlion. Although not a real animal, the Merlion is highly symbolic in Singapore. The Merlion is a combination of a lion and fish, which represents the fact that Singapore was originally a fishing village. The lion represents the original, non-Anglicized name, Singapura or the 'Lion City.'

Other than this important national animal, there are multiple other animal mascots that are easily recognized as belonging to Singapore. Let me tell you about some of them.

Can you recognize an old name of Singapore from this list?

1. Malaysia
2. Temasek
3. Indonesia

(Answer – 2. Temasek) meaning 'Sea Town.'

Iconic Animal Mascots of Singapore

Singa, the Lion — Singa has been the most recognizable mascot of Singapore. Used extensively for public education campaigns since 1982, this mascot stands for kindness, courtesy, and graciousness, all three of which are important personality traits for the people of Singapore.

Captain Green — This cute little mascot was introduced in 1990 to celebrate the 'Clean and Green' Week in the country. Since then, Captain Green has come to represent the importance of environmental preservation. The frog was chosen for this mascot because these animals are highly sensitive to environmental changes.

National bird — The national bird of Singapore is the Crimson Sunbird. In May 2002, the people of Singapore were invited to vote for their choice of the country's national bird. The Crimson Sunbird won the contest and was given the important position.

National flower — Vanda Miss Joaquim was voted the country's national flower in 1981. This flower is a hybrid orchid created by cross-breeding two different species of flowers in the 1890s. You can find this flower printed on currency notes, coins, souvenirs, etc.

Currency of Singapore

The currency of my country is the Singapore Dollar which has the same $ symbol as the US Dollar. The short form of Singapore Dollar used globally is SGD. 1 SGD = 100 cents. Here are fun and interesting facts from the currency of my country.

The currency notes have the picture of the first President of Singapore, Yusof bin Ishak, who served from 1965 to 1970.

• At the top of all Singapore currency notes, you can see 'Singapore' written in four different languages.

• A tree is printed on the $5 note that is a drawing of a real 200-year-old Tembusu tree and not a figment of any designer's imagination. This heritage botanical marvel is believed to be older than the Botanic Garden on which it stands.

• All currency notes are made with polymer because they are tear resistant and last for a longer time than ordinary currency paper. Also, it is easy to put in more security features to prevent thieves from counterfeiting our notes.

• All Singapore currency notes are Braille-friendly which means even the visually impaired people can make out the different denominations correctly.

• The largest coin in Singapore is the $80 coin, which weighs 1 kilogram (2.2 pounds).

• The SGD 10,000 currency is one of the most valuable notes in the world. The SGD 10,000 note printing was stopped in 2014. However, the currency note is still legal tender

Which note has the entire lyrics of Singapore's national anthem printed on it?

1. The $100 note
2. The $50 note
3. The $1000 note ✓

(Answer – 3. The $1000 note)

Singapore currencies can be spent as legal tender in one other country. Can you guess the country?

1. Japan
2. Brunei ✓
3. Indonesia

(Answer – 2. Brunei)

An agreement between the governments of Brunei and Singapore allow the Singapore Dollar to be used in Brunei and vice versa.

Wow, there are so many interesting and fun facts about the currency of Singapore, right? Now, let us go to some common aspects of money. Here are some of the costs of everyday items just to give you an idea:

1 liter of whole-fat milk – SGD 3.10
1 loaf of ordinary white bread – SGD 2.30
A pair of name-brand jeans – SGD 95

CHAPTER 2
WEATHER IN SINGAPORE

Spring in Singapore

In April, the weather gets hotter than in March, and you can see a lot of foggy days. Also, in April, there are frequent thunderstorms. May is similar to April except that the rains don't last very long and end abruptly. The climate in May is hot and humid.

March is comparatively cool, and you can enjoy nature walks and walks in the parks as the heat quotient is not very bad. Rains are also not very frequent though short, heavy showers do happen.

Lasting for March, April, and May, spring in Singapore is warm with less rain than in summer months. If you want a good tan, then this is the best time to visit Singapore and swim in the comforting warm waters.

Summer in Singapore

Singapore skyline in summer

Summer in Singapore lasts for three months including June, July, and August. The weather is drier in summer than during the other months. Rainfall decreases and heat increases. No one really tries to sunbathe during the month of June and July because the heat can be quite cruel and scorching. In July, rains almost stop completely, and you might get five or six days of rain in the month. August is not as hot as June and July, although it might not get very cool. However, August witnesses a lot more rain than June and July.

The rainfall during the months of September, October, and November increase significantly, especially in the last two months. Rainfall in October and November are often accompanied by thunderstorms.

The rain continues from December to January but with significantly less thunderstorms. February to March has little to no rain. The temperature also becomes cooler and more pleasant around this time.

Packing List for Singapore

Considering that the weather is more or less uniform throughout the year, here are some things you must include in your packing list while traveling to Singapore.

CHAPTER 3
HISTORY OF SINGAPORE

In the 14th century, a Sumatran prince, Sang Nila Utama, is believed to have ruled over Singapore, and he was the one who gave the country its name. According to legends, he spotted a strange and fearsome animal when he landed here.

Based on his description, his advisors told him that he had seen a lion. The prince thought it was a good omen and found the city of Singapura or the 'Lion City.'

However, there are no lions in Singapore, only tigers. Until the 1930s, tigers were seen in the forests of my country, but you can see tigers only in our zoos now.

Pop Quiz!

Can you recall from which language Singapore got its name?

1. Sanskrit ✓
2. Malay
3. Chinese

(Answer – 1. Sanskrit)

Before this legend, Chinese and Indian traders had passed through the waters around Singapore since the fifth century. Between the seventh and the tenth centuries, Singapore was under the influence and control of the ancient Buddhist kingdom of Sri Vijaya, which had its main seat of power in Sumatra.

By the thirteenth century, Islam overpowered the kingdom of Sri Vijaya, and all its regions came under the control of the Muslim empire in Malacca (or Melaka). Malacca, situated on the western coast of the Malaysian Peninsula, was a powerful and thriving seaport and commercial area.

The Muslim empire of Malacca began to decline when the Portuguese arrived at the beginning of the sixteenth century.

The Muslim traders and merchants who were responsible for the commercial success of the Muslim empire of Malacca fled from the Catholic rule of Portuguese, and a much smaller kingdom set itself up in Johor at the southern part of the Malayan Peninsula. Then, the Dutch came in 1614 followed by the English in 1875.

Early Beginnings of Modern Singapore

Stamford Raffles is credited with the founding of and laying the foundation of modern-day Singapore.

He joined as a clerk in the British East India Company in 1795. He received multiple promotions, and in 1805, he was posted in Penang. By 1811, he was made Lieutenant Governor of Java.

In 1819, he landed on the island of Singapore with the intention of setting up a base for his company in the Straits of Melaka. At that time, Singapore was made up of swamps and jungles with a very small population. However, Sir Stamford Raffles realized that this place could be a very useful port for the British East India Company.

Statue of Sir Stamford Raffles in front of Victoria Theater and Concert Hall in Singapore.

When Raffles landed, Singapore was controlled by the Empire of Johor. After the old Sultan's death, his two sons were fighting for supremacy over Johor. Raffles recognized the elder son, Hussein, as the Sultan.

He made a deal with the Sultan to get Singapore for a yearly payment. In 1824, Singapore was completely handed over to the British East India Company for a lump sum payment. Raffles became the first Resident of Singapore.

Very soon, under the supervision and residency of Sir Stamford Raffles, Singapore developed into a busy port, attracting immigrants from Malaysia, China, India, and even as far west as the Middle East!

With so many people pouring into Singapore, plans for building a town with residential and business districts were laid out, again under the supervision of Raffles.

A hill was flattened to create a business area, which is today the prestigious Shenton Way. Fort Canning became an important area, too, as many government buildings were constructed there.

In 1826, Singapore joined Melaka and Penang to become part of the British Straits Settlements, which were controlled by the British East India Company in Calcutta, India.

In 1867, the British East India Company handed over the control of Singapore directly to the British crown. Numerous monuments and buildings were constructed after this including multiple Hindu and Buddhist temples, churches, and mosques.

Sri Mariamman Temple, built in 1827 and renovated and modified in 1862, still stands tall and attracts local worshippers and international tourists.

Suez Canal Trading

Before the opening of this canal in 1869, ships had to go around the African Cape to travel between Europe and Asia. When the Suez Canal became operational, trade between Europe and Asia increased significantly because it reduced travel time for ships considerably.

Singapore, which was already becoming an important trading port in Asia, gained even more importance resulting in increased trade happening through its port. In fact, to facilitate the increased trading that took place after the opening of the Suez Canal, Singapore shifted its trading port from Boat Quay to Keppel Harbor, which was called New Harbor then.

A connection between the construction of the Suez Canal and the growth and development of Singapore exists. Do you know the names of the water bodies that the Suez Canal connects?

1. The Red Sea and the Mediterranean Sea ✓
2. The Caspian Sea and the Red Sea
3. The Red Sea and the Indian Ocean

(Answer – 1. The Red Sea and the Mediterranean Sea)

Singapore in the 20th Century

During the early part of the 20th century, Singapore's prosperity continually increased. Many Chinese immigrants landed here and made Singapore their home. Rubber and tin from the Southeast Asian regions were exported from Singapore. In January 1942, the Japanese conquered Singapore.

This political party became a strong contender in Singapore, and a new constitution was established in 1955. Lee Kuan Yew became the prime minister of Singapore, and he remained in that post until 1990.

In 1963, Singapore reunited with Malaysia. But, this reunion did not last long, and by 1965, Singapore became fully independent.

From 1965 to 1990, Singapore rose rapidly in economic and trade. By the 1990s, Singapore became a newly industrialized country. Singaporeans have a high standard of living. The rule under Lee Kuan Yew was highly authoritarian, and the society at that time was highly controlled and strict.

In 1990, Lee Kuan Yew resigned, and Goh Chok Tong, who became the prime minister, set up a more liberal regime than Lee Kuan Yew.

What did Japan call Singapore?
1. Singapore
2. Yonan
3. Temasek

(Answer – 2. Yonan)

The Singapore of Today

Today, Singapore is a highly developed nation with a thriving economy. A busy port with a population of over 5.5 million, the island-state is rapidly gaining a name for manufacturing, and continues to be the busiest port in the world.

Other thriving businesses in Singapore are oil refining, manufacture of electronic equipments, shipbuilding, repair and maintenance, and finance and banking. This small island-state is home to over 130 banks. Singapore is a leading center for both pleasure and business!

CHAPTER 4
CULTURE AND TRADITION

Political stability and economic prosperity form the foundation of the national culture in Singapore. 'Kiasu' culture is commonly associated with Singaporeans.

Kiasu literally translates to 'afraid to lose' and refers to a desire to come out in flying colors in everything we do ranging from school competitions to business negotiations.

Languages of Singapore

Singapore is a melting pot of various cultures as people from different parts of the globe have made this beautiful country their home.

Therefore, we have four official languages:

English, Mandarin, Tamil, and Malay. English is the most commonly used language in my country, as it connects people from different ethnic groups. All children learn English in school along with their mother tongue, which could be one of the four languages in the country.

Many Singaporeans also use Singlish, which is a slang combination of English and the other three languages used in Singapore!

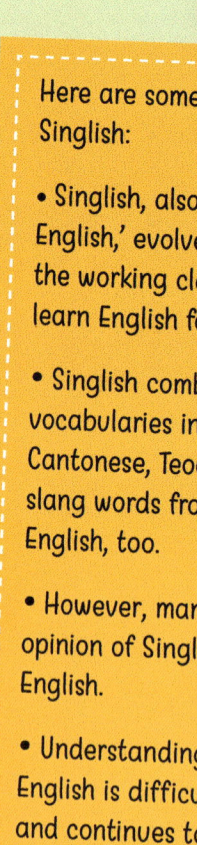

Here are some more interesting facts about Singlish:

• Singlish, also called 'Colloquial Singaporean English,' evolved when English was spoken by the working class of Singaporeans who did not learn English formally.

• Singlish combines words from different vocabularies including English, Hokkien, Malay, Cantonese, Teochew, and Tamil, and even a few slang words from American and Australian English, too.

• However, many Singaporeans have a low opinion of Singlish and prefer to use Standard English.

• Understanding Singlish by speakers of normal English is difficult. However, it is very popular and continues to be used by many people.

Religions in Singapore

Singapore believes in religious freedom, and people are free to practice their own faiths and beliefs. The primary religions include Buddhism, Islam, Christianity, Taoism, and Hinduism.

While the majority of the Singaporeans are Buddhists or Taoists, Christianity is also a widely-followed religion. Also, most of the Singaporeans of Indian origin are Hindus, and those of Malaysian origin are followers of Islam, also known as Muslims.

Some Singaporeans don't follow any religion and call themselves as free thinkers. Another beautiful and wonderful thing about religious tolerance in Singapore is that you will find Hindu temples, Buddhist temples, churches, mosques, and Taoism temples built side-by-side and everyone living in perfect harmony.

Festivals in Singapore and National Holidays

In Singapore, people celebrate the festivals of all religions with gusto. Let me give you an idea of the national holidays and important festivals celebrated in Singapore.

New Year's Day — Each new year is celebrated with a lot of pomp and show. Countdown parties take place all over the island-country in public places. The two most popular countdown parties take place at the Sentosa Island called Siloso Beach Party and in downtown Singapore called The Marina Bay Singapore Countdown. On New Year's Eve, nearly all Singaporeans attend one of these two popular public parties to enjoy some great public performances and also witness an astounding fireworks display. You can also find other New Year's Eve party places along Clarke Quay, Orchard Road, and Boat Quay.

Chinese New Year — Celebrations start on the first day of the first month of the lunar calendar. Typically, it comes between the end of January and beginning of February. This festival is so important in Singapore that preparations begin weeks before, and the entire island-state wears a beautiful, festive look.

Chinese New Year festival at night

Most families participate in other activities during the Chinese New Year such as gifting small Mandarin trees, which stand for prosperity, and also visiting temples to pray for a happy, prosperous year.

Chinatown, an area in Singapore that has a dense Chinese population, is the place to visit during this time. The streets are lined with Chinese lanterns and spectacular decorations. The lion and dragon dances take place in Chinatown as well as along the banks of the Singapore River.

Crowd at Guan Yin Temple In Singapore during Vesak Day

Vesak Day — Vesak Day falls on the full moon day of the 4th lunar month. This day is the most important annual event for the followers of Buddhism and commemorates the three important events in the life of Buddha namely his birth, enlightenment, and his final nirvana or liberation.

- Public talks about Buddhism
- Vegetarian food fairs
- Singing of hymns

Even though Vesak Day is celebrated with a lot of reverence and respect, it is a quieter and calmer festival than most others in Singapore.

Singapore National Day Military Parade

National Day — This important day in Singapore falls on August 9th and commemorates the country's independence. A much-awaited National Day Parade takes place every year, which is watched by more than 25000 spectators.

The National Day Parade is held at the Marina Bay and has a lot of activities including fun and comic shows, and of course, the actual parade. Other ceremonies include the Presidential Gun Salute, and finally, the parade ends with an impressive display of fireworks.

Hari Raya Puasa — This festival is called Eid Ul Fitr in the rest of the world. Hari Raya Puasa is an important festival for Malays, the majority of whom are Muslims. This festival falls on the last day of the holy month of Ramadan, which is spent in fasting and prayer.

Geylang Serai is the center of the Malay community, and this place is lit up and decorated beautifully for Hari Raya Puasa.

Deepavali — Also called 'Festival of Lights,' Deepavali is the most important religious festival for Hindus. Deepavali typically falls in October/November. Preparations begin weeks before the actual festival day with the streets of Little India (an area in Singapore that is populated by the Indian ethnic community) adorned and decorated with flowers and lights. Roadside shops sell colorful earthen lamps, and sweetmeat shops sell a big variety of amazingly mouthwatering Indian sweets. Singapore bans fireworks for Deepavali, so people gather together in the evening and light sparklers in their respective communities.

Hari Raya Haji — Called Eid Al Adha, or Feast of Sacrifice, Hari Raya Haji is an important day on the Muslim calendar that marks the end of the holy Haj pilgrimage period. The festival falls in November or December, and most of the celebrations are similar to what happens during Hari Raya Puasa.

Christmas Day — The Christmas period is the most beautiful and enchanting time in Singapore. A Christmas extravaganza that lasts seven weeks takes place every year in my country. Called 'Christmas in the Tropics,' this festive period starts from the end of November and lasts into the first week of January.

The Marina Bay and Orchard Road areas are transformed into fairylands with grand arches, festive street lightings, themed settings, and some stunning water features. This entire project of lighting and decorations in Singapore for the Christmas period is famous as 'Christmas Light-Up.'

Other Important Religious Festivals

Hungry Ghost Festival — This important Chinese festival is celebrated on the first day of the seventh month in the lunar calendar, which is also referred to as the Ghost Month. It is celebrated on the fourteenth or fifteenth day of this Ghost Month, which falls usually in the middle of August. There are two quite contradictory (which means opposite to each other) versions to the story of the Hungry Ghost Festival.

Mooncake Festival – This festival has many names including Mid-Autumn Festival and Zhong Qiu Jie in Mandarin. This holiday is celebrated on the fifteenth day of the eighth lunar month, which usually falls in mid-September.

Moon-viewing parties are one of the most common activities on this day. People sit in gardens that are lit up with beautiful lanterns watching the moon, sipping tea, and nibbling on mooncakes. Mooncakes are delicious cakes made with lotus seed or red bean paste and egg yolk.

Let me tell you an interesting story behind the Mooncake Festival:

Long, long ago, there lived a cruel king called Hou Yi. He had the elixir of life, which he wanted to drink to become immortal but his wife, Chang'e, decided to save the people of the kingdom from his tyrannical rule. She stole the elixir of life and ascended to the moon and began to be worshipped as the Moon Goddess.

Hou Yi was given the mooncake and sent to live in the sun. The special cake he ate gave him the strength to withstand the sun's scorching heat. On the fifteenth day of the eighth lunar month every year, Hou Yi visited his wife on the moon. The Mooncake Festival is a celebration of that annual reunion.

Thaipusam Festival – This festival, which usually comes in the month of January/February, is a day of thanksgiving for followers of Hinduism. Hindus celebrate and thank the gods for the fulfillment of their vows.

A big procession of devotees travels from Sri Srinivasa Perumal Temple to the Sri Thendayuthapani Temple, a distance of 4 km (about 2.5 miles). The Thaipusam Festival is celebrated with a lot of religious fervor in Singapore.

If you are a visitor to Singapore, then it is best for you to know these customs that may or may not be in your home country.

Other Customs and Traditions of Singapore

The family is the central unit of the social structure – Respect and loyalty start at home with elders getting preferential seating arrangements and also getting to be introduced first.

Singaporeans take cleanliness very seriously – I am proud to say that Singapore is one of the cleanest countries in the world. You only have to walk into Changi International Airport and you will see how seriously we take cleanliness. Every single inch of the airport is constantly cleaned and polished.

The city is spotlessly clean everywhere you go. Littering is strictly forbidden and attract hefty fines. Chewing gum is not allowed in my country. The only way you can legally buy and chew gum is if you have a prescription from your dentist.

Take off your shoes before entering a home – This custom is followed nearly in all homes in my country. You must remember to remove your shoes and footwear and leave them close to the door. Some homes have shoe racks for this purpose.

Lines are strictly followed in Singapore Singaporeans queue up for everything including to buy food from the street hawker, order at MacDonald's or KFC outlets, to buy tickets for a movie, to get into a bus or train, or anything else. Following lines is a strictly followed concept in Singapore, and it would be upsetting if people do not stick to lines.

Address all elderly people as uncle/aunty — This address is of the most common ways of showing respect to the elderly in Singapore. As a child, if you get into a cab and want to give instructions to the cab driver, then you must say, 'Uncle, please take to me to [the name of your destination].'

Give up reserved seats

Trains and buses have seats reserved for the elderly, pregnant women, handicapped people, and young children. If you do occupy such a seat when the carriage is empty, you must give it up if a person qualified for the seat walks in. In fact, local Singaporeans will not even occupy such seats, even if the carriage is empty.

Tipping is not allowed in Singapore

Most foreign visitors are used to tipping waiters. However, in Singapore, there is no need for tipping, and is, in fact, frowned upon as restaurant bills include service tax.

Slow movers have to keep to the left of the road

While you might be used to this rule when it comes to vehicles, in Singapore, this has to be followed for pedestrians too. Pedestrians are people moving on foot or walking on the streets. So, if you are a slow walker, keep to the left of the road.

Popular Foods

The staple foods in Singapore are rice, chicken, fish, and vegetables. We make multiple varieties of dishes using these four basic staples and seasoning them with different spices like coconut, chilis, tamarind, and lime. Many Singaporeans eat outside their homes in different centers where food is freshly made and very cheap too. Also, you will find many restaurants, cafes, coffeehouses, and teahouses serving a multitude of cuisines from different countries.

We use forks and spoons like westerners but when eating Chinese dishes, we always use chopsticks, and when eating Indian or Malay food, we often use our fingers. As Singapore consists of diverse races and religions, there are a variety of eating habits you will see. For example, Singaporeans of Indian origin don't eat beef while those of Malay origin don't eat pork. Some of the Buddhist Chinese follow vegetarianism on certain days of the week or month and also on certain festivals.

Roti prata — Nothing like this comfort food after a day of hectic sightseeing in Singapore. This Indian flatbread has fillings of your choice. You can wash the dish down with some amazing Teh Tarik, also called pulled hot milk tea.

Rojak — Rojak is a yummy Asian version of the English salad, made with cucumbers, roasted peanuts, cut fruits, and some fried dough fritters. The fritters are an essential ingredient while the rest can be mixed and matched according to your taste. Don't forget to try a plate, I'm sure you will not be able to stop at one!

Kaya toast — This dish is an unmissable Singaporean breakfast staple consisting of thin toasted crispy bread layered with butter and coconut jam and served with 2 half-boiled eggs. Nothing can start your day better than Kaya toast.

Pandan cake — Pandan cake is fluffy, light, sweet, and perfect for a mid-day snack.

Nasi lemak — Translating to 'fat rice,' nasi lemak is a rice dish cooked in coconut milk, topped with fried egg, chicken, prawns, and cucumbers. It's great for breakfast and dinner!

Satay — Eaten with sweet, spicy peanut sauce, satay is skewered and grilled meat served on sticks, eaten with diced cucumbers and rice cakes on the side.

Laksa — This dish is a rich rice noodle dish served with prawns and other seafood items.

Bak kut teh — This amazing, delicious dish is made with pork ribs cooked in a spicy peppery broth.

> The food items available in Singapore will leave you wanting for more. Don't forget to try all the items mentioned here.

CHAPTER 5
NATIVE PLANTS AND ANIMALS

Currently, forest area covers only about 28 square km (10 square miles) of land. Many plants, sea animals, and land animals native to this island disappeared because of land reclamation (which means converting existing forestland and water areas into land suitable for housing and farming) as more and more people came to make Singapore their home.

Before the urbanization of Singapore, which started back in 1819 by Stamford Raffles, the entire area of the island was covered in dense forest land. Thick mangrove swamps and rainforests were found in the center of the island-state.

The urbanization and increasing number of immigrants to this beautiful and prosperous island resulted in near-complete deforestation of the area.

Today, mangroves are restricted to the northern parts of the main island and in smaller isles such as Pulau Ubin, Pulau Semakau, and Pulau Tekong. Evergreen rainforests are found in the Bukit Timah Nature Reserve.

However, despite the urbanization of the country, the government works hard to preserve and protect forest areas and flora and fauna in them. There are more than 3000 hectares (over 7000 acres) of forest reserves including:

• The Sungei Buloh Wetland Reserve

• The Labrador Nature Reserve

• The Central Catchment Nature Reserve

• The Bukit Timah Nature Reserve

Animals Found in of Singapore

Otters — Otters can be found in the Marina Bay area, Pulau Ubin, and also a pair in the Bishan-Ang Mo Kio Park. Although they are cute, they are wild animals and should be treated with care. Feeding them and fooling around with them are totally forbidden.

Mouse-deer — Another animal unique to Singapore, the mouse-deer is assumed to be very smart and intelligent and can outsmart more dangerous and larger animals.

We even have a fable about a clever mouse-deer who wanted to cross a river full of dangerous crocodiles. It tricked the crocodiles into forming a single line across the river so that it can go to the other side.

Pretty cunning, right!

Dolphins — You can find hordes of these cute animals in Singapore Strait, especially the pink and bottlenose dolphins. If you are lucky, then you can also get to see them while traveling to Sisters' Islands.

Porcupines — For a long time, the Malayan porcupine, which people believe is native to Singapore had not been seen, and it was thought they had disappeared from this island-country. Thanks to advanced cameras set up in the forest areas of Pulau Ubin and Pulau Tekong, we know that these unique creatures are still in Singapore!

Green-crested lizards – Sporting an intense dark green body that turns brown when stressed, these lizards are quite a sight to see. They are found in Sungei Buloh Wetland Reserve, Central Catchment Nature Reserve, Singapore Botanic Gardens, and Pulau Tekong.

Flying lemurs – These cute, cuddly creatures, which carry their young ones on their backs, can glide up to a distance of 100 m. They are found in abundance in the Central Catchment Nature Reserve and Bukit Timah Nature Reserve.

Dugongs – Also known as sea cows, dugongs are the gentle giants of the sea. They eat seagrass and are happy on their own. Can you guess the name of the animal after which dewgongs in the Pokemon TV series are named after?

Cobras – Only one highly venomous species of cobra is found in Singapore. Eating frogs and rodents, cobras strike humans only if we go too close for their comfort. They are a common sight and you can see them in parks and gardens.

Crocodiles – Crocodiles are found in the swamplands of Sungei Buloh. In fact, there is a crocodile viewing spot from where you can catch sight of one or two crocodiles if you are patient and willing to wait.

Naked bulldog bats — Like all bats, the naked bulldog bats are seen only in the night. They eat insects and make a unique yawning sound. You can find them in the Bukit Timah Nature Reserve.

White-bellied blind snakes — The strange thing about this non-venomous snake is that its front and back look similar. But, if you look closely one end looks like a human toenail. Remember that toenail-like part is the front-end. These creepy-crawlies are seen in the Central Catchment Nature Reserve and Pulau Ubin.

These creatures are quite shy and avoid contact with human beings. However, if they feel threatened, then they can strike you with their tails, which are so powerful that they can fracture a bone in an adult.

Long-tailed macaque
As these poor monkeys have lost their forest homes because of deforestation, they are moving into our homes. You can find them in many public places. The most important thing to remember is not to feed them or try to irritate them in any way. If you leave them alone, they are quite fine. Otherwise, they can get aggressive.

Mynas and crows
The common birds that you will find all over Singapore as you take a walk on the streets include the Javan Myna (easily recognizable by its yellow beak and black and brown feathers) and the House Crow which is completely black including its beak.

Ant-snatching assassin bugs — These creatures prey on ants, and they stick the bodies of the ants they have killed on to their backs as camouflage. The dead ants hide their own smell and allow them to infiltrate and attack ant colonies for more food.

Finless sleeper rays — They live on the ocean floors around Singapore. Unlike other sting-ray fishes, the finless sleeper rays give a mild electric shock if you try to touch them.

Plant Life in Singapore

Despite the small size of my country, I am proud to say that we have more than 2200 plant species that are recorded and registered. Many of these native plants do not flower or blossom like the ones that have been imported from foreign countries.

Still, it makes sense to tell you about my native plants first and then talk about other common plants such as the bougainvillea that are found all over Singapore including at the Changi International Airport.

Orange spiral ginger — This plant grows very fast up to a height of 1.5 meters. The unique thing about this plant is that the exotic flowers are found very close to the ground. So, you need to look down to catch a glimpse of the beautiful flowers of the orange spiral ginger plant.

The Yellow Flame tree — Growing up to a height of 20 meters, this tree is commonly found along streets and in many green spots in the urban part of Singapore. The vibrant yellow flowers form a beautiful crown when the tree is in full bloom and create a soft carpet when they wither to the ground.

Common Dianella — When this plant is not in bloom, then it looks like a lump of long-leaved grass. However, when it is ready to bloom, a long stem grows out of this plant holding dozens of little blue-violet flowers that are a sight to see.

Aquatic ginger — These plants grow in waterlogged areas and can be seen partially submerged in water. They can be easily recognized by their small, pinkish-white flowers that appear at the tips of stems

Lipstick plant — In home gardens, the lipstick plant is grown in pots. However, in the wild, they grow on tree trunks and branches. The plant gets its name from the bright red flower buds that look like lipsticks.

Tembusu — Tembusu is one of the most majestic trees of Singapore and can grow up to a height of 40 meters. This evergreen tree has dark, dense foliage. The white flowers of this wonderful tree open during sunset and emit a sweet scent.

Which Singapore currency note has a Tembusu tree designed on it?

1. SGD100
2. SGD5
3. SGD10

(Answer – 2. SGD5)

Bougainvillea — This is one of the most common plants that you will see everywhere in Singapore. The colors of the flowers of this plant range from white to pink to orange to magenta and deep red too.

So, when a row of bougainvillea plants are found together, the burst of colors is a stunningly beautiful sight to see.

Frangipani — With deep pink or creamy white flowers, frangipani trees are found in Buddhist and Hindu temples. Local Malay communities believe that spirits live in frangipani trees, so you will find them in cemeteries and graveyards too.

CHAPTER 6
FAMOUS PEOPLE OF SINGAPORE

Many famous people have made Singaporeans proud because of their contributions to the growth and development of the country and also by sharing their talents with the rest of the world. Let us look at some of the famous people from my country.

Stamford Raffles

Stamford Raffles worked for the British East India Company, and he was sent to Southeast Asia to locate and set up a new port for the British as the other ports were controlled by the Dutch.

He surveyed the area and chose Singapore for the abundance of water and a great port location. Singapore was right in the center of the Straits of Melaka. He then laid the foundation to build a modern and urban city in that area, and that first step led to modern-day Singapore.

Raffles is so famous even today that Singaporeans have named streets, institutions, schools, colleges, and even a shopping mall after him. Here are some lesser known facts about this great man:

> How is Stamford Raffles famous in Singapore?
> 1. The founder of Singapore City ✓
> 2. The architect of Singapore
> 3. The king of Singapore
>
> (Answer – 1. The founder of Singapore City)

More Fun Facts about Stamford Raffles

• Established in 1826, one of the world's oldest zoo, the London Zoo, was the brainchild of Stamford Raffles.

• He loved nature and collected interesting and unique flora and fauna from all his travels the world over. He set up the first Botanic Garden in Singapore in 1822 around Fort Canning.

• Although he laid the foundation for a prosperous city, he had a lot of debt when he died which he means he was very poor and had no money at the time of his death.

William Farquhar

Willian Farquhar, a Scotsman by birth, played an important role in realizing Raffles's dreams of creating a beautiful and modern city from the forests and swamplands. William Farquhar had to manage and overcome challenges of setting up a new colony.

Some of these challenges included problems from pirates, slavery, and a lot of friction and conflict among the different immigrant groups. He also laid the foundation for an urban city.

A big rat menace occurred during that time on the island. William Farquhar came out with a novel scheme to quickly get rid of all the rats and rodents. He announced an award of one shilling for every rat that was killed by the people. This exercise prevented the spread of a cholera epidemic.

Yusof bin Ishak

Mr. Yusof was born on August 12, 1910. After completing his primary education at Victoria Bridge School (which is known as Victoria School today), he joined Raffles Institution.

Before he became the president of the country, he worked as a journalist and established a Malayan newspaper called Utusan Melayu. His intention was to build and develop the Malay community to which he belonged. He encouraged his community people to educate themselves.

Before he became the president of the country, he worked as a journalist and established a Malayan newspaper called Utusan Melayu. His intention was to build and develop the Malay community to which he belonged. He encouraged his community people to educate themselves.

Before he became the president of the country, he worked as a journalist and established a Malayan newspaper called Utusan Melayu. His intention was to build and develop the Malay community to which he belonged. He encouraged his community people to educate themselves.

Who was the first President of Singapore whose face is on all Singapore currency notes?

1. Stamford Raffles
2. Lee Kuan Yew
3. Yusof bin Ishak

(Answer — 3. Yusof bin Ishak)

Lee Kuan Yew

Also referred to as the Founding Father of Singapore, Lee Kuan Yew governed the country from 1959 until 1990. Yes, he led the country for three decades.

> Do you know of another nickname given to this great man?
>
> 1. The Builder of Singapore
> 2. The Architect of Modern Singapore
> 3. The Best Man in Singapore
>
> (Answer – 2. The Architect of Modern Singapore)

He dropped his English name in 1950 after leaving Cambridge. He attended the University of Cambridge where he learned law and also was a student of the London School of Economics.

He tried to combine modern urban ideas and conservation of nature to build a beautiful city while preserving nature. For example, the Marina Barrage, a dam was his idea to help in creating space for more buildings in the area. However, he also set up the Gardens by the Bay to make sure Singapore's greenery was not lost due to urbanization.

He was such a proud Singaporean that he did not miss a single National Day Parade since Singapore's independence.

He was very strict about his daily exercise. He used to exercise on his treadmill three times a day. He truly believed in the importance of health for a long, happy life.

Fun Facts about Lee Kuan Yew

- Two awards namely Lee Kuan Yew Water Prize and Lee Kuan Yew City Prize for water conservation and creation of sustainable urban environments respectively are named after him. Both these awards reflect Lee Kuan Yew's contribution to Singapore.

- He gave a lot of importance to children learning and mastering two languages (which is referred to as bilingualism). He donated 10 million dollars for this purpose.

> Can you guess what was Kuan's English name?
>
> 1. Henry
> 2. Harry
> 3. Kevin
>
> (Answer – 2. Harry)

Other important and famous people of Singapore who have made this country

Stephanie Sun — She is a world-famous singer-songwriter who is also known as Sun Yan Zi.

Zoe Tay — She is a versatile actress and a former model. She is famous as Queen of Caldecott Hill, which is the heart of the media industry in Singapore.

Fandi Ahmed — A soccer superstar from Singapore, Fandi Ahmed was a midfielder and striker during his play days and is today a famous coach.

Goh Chok Tong — He became the Prime Minister of Singapore in 1990 after Lee Kuan Yew stepped down. His political views and ideas are still sought out by the present leaders of Singapore, and he holds important advisory positions in the government.

CHAPTER 7
MAJOR ATTRACTIONS

The main island of Singapore is one of the most kid-friendly travel destinations in Asia with so many fun things to do that you will feel sad that your vacation in my beautiful country is over. You will definitely want to keep returning. Here are some of the places you simply cannot miss in Singapore.

Universal Studios Singapore

Universal Studios in Singapore is the ultimate place for theme park fun and activities. You must spend an entire day here without fail, and I am quite certain you will want to revisit it on your next trip to my country. Located on Sentosa Island, here are some amazing facts about this place.

Universal Studios Singapore measures 20 hectares (almost 50 acres), and that's really huge. The park opened in May 2011, and by January 2017, more than 25 million people had crossed the gates of this wonderful theme park. The Universal Studios Singapore Globe is the most easily recognizable element in this park. It took 40 days to build this one globe!

This amusement park has won the Best Amusement Park in Asia numerous times beating other great places such as Tokyo Disneyland, Universal Studios Japan, and Legoland Malaysia.

The roller coasters are outstanding. With plenty of options to choose from, the highest and scariest one is Human vs. Cylon Battlestar Galactica, which is 42.5 m (139 feet) high.

Gardens by the Bay

The tallest of these super trees is 16 stories, and you can make a trip right to the top and get an amazing view of the Marina Bay area and the entire landscape of the gardens.

Gardens by the Bay is a fabulous place to celebrate nature as well as the flora and fauna diversity of Singapore. This attraction has three waterfront gardens named Bay East, Bay Central, and Bay East.

The Supertree Grove in the Gardens by the Bay has huge tree-like structures with wide canopies that provide shade during the day and at night they provide an exhilarating display of lights.

Singapore Discovery Center

Located very close to the heart of the main island, Singapore Discovery Center offers a wide range of indoor and outdoor activities for kids and adults. Here are some great things you can do in this fun place.

Pedal a boat on Discovery Lake — You can rent a pedal boat and go on a leisurely ride on Discovery Lake.

Learn to be a news reporter — You can become a live news reporter, present your report on different events of Singapore, and see yourself as a journalist on TV for a while.

Play the Crossfire Paintball game — A fun game, which calls for shooting your enemies with replicas of Bravo-1 rifles to shoot paint on your enemies.

Singapore Night Safari

You can see thousands of animals from all over the world in their natural habitat in the Singapore Night Safari ride. Here are some interesting facts about this wonderful nocturnal journey of excitement and fun:

Fun Facts about the Night Safari

- The Singapore Night Safari was opened on 26 May 1994 and was built at a total cost of $63 million!

- More than 2500 animals are housed here. These animals are not the ones in the Singapore Zoo. Since the opening of the safari, many babies have been born here such as Asian elephants, Malayan tigers, Asian lions, and clouded leopards.

- The lighting arrangement in the safari is designed to replicate a full-moon scene.

- In addition to seeing a variety of night creatures, you will also get to see flowers that bloom at night including butterfly ginger, pigeon orchids, orange blossoms, and chempaka.

- You can take the tram ride through the safari or one of the four walking trails to see everything there is to see here.

Wild Wild Wet Singapore

Wild Wild Wet Singapore is the best water-theme park that is sure to blow your mind. You can ride some adrenaline-pumping rides or just sit and relax on gentle pools or flumes. Here are some water rides you must not miss here:

Vortex — This amazing water ride is a closed red slide that send you down at a speed of 10m per second giving you the thrill of your life as you end up splashing to safety at the end of the slide.

Kraken Racers — You come down a four-lane water slide on a mat. The best part of this ride is that you can slide down with your friends and have a race.

Royal Flush — This ride allows four people to sit on a raft, slide down a tunnel, and then go up a nearly straight vertical wall! Whoa! Can be quite exciting if you can manage the palpitations of your heart!

Other than these adrenaline-pumping rides, you can also enjoy some relaxing rides such as lazily floating on the Shiok River on a tube, enjoying the waves in the artificial beach or wave pool, and some kid-friendly and not-so-scary kid rides.

Singapore Flyer

Called Singapore Flyer, a huge Ferris wheel in Marina Bay gives you a bird's eye view of Singapore. At the tallest point, Singapore Flyer has a height of 165 meters (541 feet) and you will little miss from here! Here is some interesting and fun information about the Singapore Flyer:

• One of the world's largest Ferris wheels, the Flyer has a capacity to hold more than 780 people.

• The wheel has 28 fully air-conditioned capsules each of which can hold 28 passengers.

• You can even see the coasts of Indonesia and Malaysia from the topmost position of Singapore Flyer.

• In the beginning, the wheel turned in a counterclockwise direction but was later changed to the clockwise based on advice from Feng Shui experts. (Feng Shui is a Chinese system of principles involving spatial arrangements and orientation).

Jurong Bird Park

Located in Jurong Hill, this bird park is a unique and beautiful feather in Singapore tourism cap. With more 5000 birds, Jurong Bird Park is the perfect place for you to learn about and appreciate the importance of wildlife and nature.

You can use the guided tram rides, or you can rent scooters, strollers, and wagons for a fee and go on your own trip. Some important tips to follow:

• You are allowed to walk or roam around in the places earmarked for humans. You cannot enter prohibited areas.

• You should not feed, tease, and do any other kind of harmful things to the birds here. Their safety is the most important thing for the keepers of this park.

When you take a photo at the Jurong Bird Park, make sure you don't have the flash on because it can disturb or even blind the birds.

Other Islands of Singapore

Pulau Ubin — Lying northeast of the main island, Pulau Ubin is an island on which you can enjoy the beauty of nature while gorging on yummy seafood. Many locals visit this island to get a feel of village life that existed during the 1960s.

The island is known for its numerous granite quarries, which supplied this important element to the construction industry of Singapore. The granite from this island was used to build the Horsburgh Lighthouse and the Singapore-Johor causeway.

Today, none of the quarries are operational and are being filled with water or revegetation. In the 1970s, when the quarry industry saw a drop, people started leaving Pulau Ubin.

A day on this beautiful, calm island is a perfect getaway for most families in Singapore. Rent a bicycle and explore the island. You can check out the marine wildlife at Chek Jawa which are wetlands consisting of sandy and rocky shores and mangroves.

> During low tide, you can see small marine creatures such as crabs and mudskippers. You can take a guided walking tour to delve deeper into the wildlife of Pulau Ubin.
>
> House No.1 in Pulau Ubin is a structure built in the 1930s, and even today, the fireplace in this Tudor-style home works.

Pulau Hantu — Hantu translates to 'ghost' in Malay, and so, Pulau Hantu means 'island of ghosts.' A legend attached to these islands states the Malayan people believe that ancient warriors dueled on this island and died, and their ghosts still wander around this beautiful little isle.

This beautiful island is only 30 minutes away by boat and is very popular among the locals and tourists for swimming, fishing, scuba diving, and snorkeling.

This island is bordered by little coral reefs in which you can get to see a variety of marine life including butterfly fish, crabs, clownfish, sea slugs, octopuses, and, if you are lucky, you might get to see seahorses too.

Of course, today, Pulau Hantu is one of the best and most peaceful places to get away for a day from the hustle and bustle of the city. Rich reefs, white sands, and swaying palms welcome you. No one has sighted any ghosts!

Sisters' Islands – Located to the south of the main island, Sisters' Islands along with the surrounding waters is referred to as the country's first marine park. Here is an interesting story behind these cute, little islands.

So, Sisters' Islands consists of two islets including Big Sister's Island or Pulau Subar Laut, and Little Sister's Island or Pulau Subar Darat. The big island is about 3.9 hectares (9 acres) while the smaller one is 1.7 hectares (4 acres). Even today, people believe that every year on the day the islands were formed, a huge thunderstorm with heavy rainfall hits.

Long, long ago, there lived two sisters called Minah and Lina who loved each other very much and could not bear to be separated. Now, a pirate came into their lives and wanted to marry the younger sister, Lina. But, she said no to him because she did not want to be separated from her beloved sister.

The pirate kidnapped Lina and took her away to his boat. Minah jumped into the water hoping to save her little sister, but she started drowning. Lina saw her sister struggling in the water, freed herself from the pirate, and jumped into the water too.

Then, a large wave hit, and everyone in the story died. After the storm had subsided, the sisters were not to be seen. But, two islands emerged at the place where they drowned.

Sisters' Islands is home to the Marine Park, which is a huge 40 hectare (almost 100 acres) of land water surrounding these two islands and extendin g to the seashores of nearby islands of Pulau Tekukor and St. John's Island.

The Sisters' Islands Marine Park protects Singapore's coral reefs, a unique ecosystem that is home to rare species of seahorses and other marine life including clams, crabs, etc. You can go on guided walking tours, which are free of cost, and learn about the beauty and wonder of marine life in this area.

Conclusion

That brings us to the end of our Singapore trip. I hope you loved traveling through my beautiful country and reading about its wonderful stories and facts. I would like to end our trip with a little quiz on Singapore to help you recall some important places, events, and people. But before that, can you answer the following questions:

Which part(s) of the Singapore travel did you like the most and why?

_____
_____
_____
_____
_____
_____

What activities did you enjoy most and why?

_____
_____
_____
_____
_____
_____

Now, to the Singapore quiz.

What was the original name of Singapore?

1. It was always known as Singapore
2. Temasek
3. Johor

(Answer – 2. Temasek)

What is the name of the Sumatran prince who gave the name of Singapore?

1. Srivijaya
2. Sang Nila Utama
3. Skanda Shah

(Answer – 2. Sang Nila Utama)

In which year did Singapore become completely independent?

1. 1961
2. 1950
3. 1963

(Answer – 3. 1963)

Pulau Ubin provided an important element to the construction industry of Singapore. What was that item?
1. Fish
2. Sand
3. Granite

(Answer – 3. Granite)

What is the height of the tallest peak in Singapore, Bukit Timah Hill?

1. 1000 ft
2. 540 ft
3. 300 ft

(Answer – 2. 540 ft)

What is the meaning of the Sanskrit word Singapura from which Singapore is derived?

1. Tiger City
2. Elephant City
3. Lion City

(Answer – 3. Lion City)

From 1942 to 1945, Singapore was under the control of which country?

1. USA
2. China
3. Japan

(Answer – 3. Japan)

Who was the first Prime Minister of Singapore?

1. Lee Kuan Yew
2. Goh Chok Tong
3. Singapore has only a president

(Answer – 1. Lee Kuan Yew)

What is the language of the instruction in Singaporean schools?

1. Malay
2. English
3. Chinese

(Answer – 2. English)

How many islands make up the country of Singapore?

1. 100
2. 2
3. 63

(Answer – 3. 63)

Who is responsible for establishing modern Singapore?

1. William Farquhar
2. Stamford Raffles
3. John Crawford

(Answer – 2. Stamford Raffles)

I hope I was able to trigger some memories from your Singapore trip with this quiz. I would be wonderful to have you visit us again.